Law Enforcement

Mounted Police

by Michael Green

Content Consultant:
Sergeant Divo Martini (retired)
New York City Police Department Mounted Unit

RiverFront Books

An Imprint of Franklin Watts
A Division of Grolier Publishing
New York   London   Hong Kong   Sydney
Danbury, Connecticut

RiverFront Books
http://publishing.grolier.com
Copyright © 1998 Capstone Press. All rights reserved. Published
simultaneously in Canada. No part of this book may be reproduced without
written permission from the publisher. The publisher takes no responsibility
for the use of any of the materials or methods described in this book, nor for
the products thereof. Printed in the United States of America.

Library of Congress Cataloging-in-Publication Data
Green, Michael, 1952-
    Mounted police/by Michael Green.
    p. cm. -- (Law enforcement)
    Includes bibliographical references.
    Summary: Presents a brief history of mounted police; describes their
functions, horses, uniforms, and equipment; and gives particular attention to
the New York City mounted unit.
    ISBN 1-56065-757-X
    1. Mounted police--Juvenile literature. 2. Police horses--Juvenile
literature. [1. Mounted police. 2. Police horses. 3. Police. 4. Horses.]
I. Title. II. Series: Green, Michael, 1952- Law enforcement.

HV7922.G722 1998
363.2'32--dc21

                                                97-40393
                                                CIP
                                                AC

Editorial credits
Editor, Timothy Larson; cover design, Timothy Halldin; photo research,
    Michelle L. Norstad
Photo credits
California Highway Patrol, 23
Michael Green, 4, 6, 16, 18, 20, 24, 26, 28, 30, 33, 34, 36, 38, 47
New York City Police Department, cover, 8, 10, 12
Leslie O'Shaughnessy, 41
Royal Canadian Mounted Police, 15

Table of Contents

Chapter 1

Mounted Police Units

A mounted police unit is a group of officers that works on horseback. Mounted police units have a long history in the United States. Officers rode horses before the invention of automobiles. Officers needed horses to pull police wagons and carriages. A carriage is a small, two-wheeled coach.

In the 1920s, police departments replaced many of their horses with automobiles. Police officers used automobiles for most police business. Automobiles allowed officers to cover large areas and to travel quickly.

Today, automobiles are the main form of police transportation. Transportation is all the ways of moving people and goods. But more than

Mounted police officers work on horseback.

650 law enforcement agencies still have mounted units. A law enforcement agency is an office or department that makes sure people obey laws.

Duties

Mounted units work to make citizens feel safe. They perform many jobs. Mounted units patrol busy streets and city parks. They control crowds. They keep order at large events like concerts. They lead parades. They help on search and rescue operations. Some mounted units patrol city beaches.

Mounted units also help people trust police and learn about police work. While on duty, mounted officers talk with people. They answer questions about their horses and their jobs.

Some mounted units hold riding shows for the public. Officers perform drills during these shows. The drills let officers display their skills and the skills of their horses.

Mounted officers answer questions about their horses and their jobs.

Chapter 2

History

The idea for mounted police units started in England more than 300 years ago. Many cities and towns in England did not have police departments. Instead, sheriffs and deputies patrolled towns and cities. A deputy is a law enforcement officer who works for a sheriff. Sheriffs and their deputies traveled on horseback.

In the early 1600s, English colonists brought the idea of mounted sheriffs to America. Colonists are people who settle in distant lands but remain governed by their native countries.

Mounted sheriffs and their deputies patrolled towns and cities in the American colonies. The state governments formed county sheriffs departments after the Revolutionary War (1775-1783). Most of the sheriffs departments

The idea for today's mounted police units started in England more than 300 years ago.

The NYPD formed its first mounted unit in 1871.

continued to use horses until the 1920s and 1930s.

In the 1970s, a few sheriffs departments formed special mounted units. The units are still in service today. Many of the units are made up of officers who volunteer to serve. Volunteer means to offer to do a job. The volunteer officers supply their own horses and equipment.

Mounted Police Units

In 1845, New York became one of the first cities to form a police department. In 1871, the New York Police Department (NYPD) organized a mounted unit. It was the first U.S. police department to form a mounted unit.

The Canadian government formed the Royal Canadian Mounted Police (RCMP) in 1873. The RCMP may be the best-known mounted police force. The RCMP has been the subject of many movies, television programs, and books.

The NYPD Mounted Unit

In 1871, the NYPD needed help controlling the city's busy streets. Galloping horses and fast-moving carriages and wagons were a danger in the crowded city. Many people died in horse-related accidents. Police officers who patrolled on foot could not control the problem. So the NYPD formed the Mounted Unit to help solve the problem.

The NYPD Mounted Unit had 13 officers and 15 horses. In its first year, the mounted unit made 429 arrests. The number of street accidents

Today, the NYPD Mounted Unit includes more than 145 officers and 100 horses.

decreased. The mounted unit quickly grew in size. By 1901, the mounted unit had about 700 horses and officers.

The NYPD Mounted Unit took on new duties as it grew. The unit led parades. The officers and their horses cleared the way for parade marchers and floats. The mounted unit also became responsible for controlling crowds. Mounted officers could look down into crowds and spot problems easily.

The unit grew and shrank many times over the years. By 1976, financial problems almost forced the unit to shut down. New York City had no money to care for the unit's horses. It could not afford supplies and equipment. Businesses and individuals saved the unit. They gave money, horses, and supplies.

The NYPD Mounted Unit Today

The NYPD Mounted Unit now includes more than 145 officers and 100 horses. Many of the officers and horses serve in six troops. The troops are Troops A through F. Each troop has a stable located in a different part of the city. A stable is a barn for horses. Some of the officers serve at the Mounted Unit Headquarters.

The unit still patrols New York's busy streets. Mounted officers control traffic and crowds. Traffic is moving trucks, buses, and cars. Mounted officers lead parades and help protect important people who visit the city. The unit also holds a riding show.

The Royal Canadian Mounted Police

The North West Mounted Police was the original name of the Royal Canadian Mounted Police. The

Canadian government formed this police force to help settle northern and western Canada. These territories were wilderness areas. Only a few hunters, trappers and native people lived there.

The mounted police wore bright red uniforms and traveled on horseback. The Canadian government sent the mounted police into the territories before the settlers arrived. The mounted police officers worked to make peace with native peoples. They also made sure people obeyed Canadian laws.

In 1920, the Canadian government changed the force's name to the Royal Canadian Mounted Police. The RCMP became Canada's main law enforcement agency. It enforced laws in most of Canada's provinces. A province is a region similar to a state. The RCMP helped protect Canada's borders. Many officers also served in military units during World War II (1939-1945).

The RCMP Today

The Royal Canadian Mounted Police now enforce local, national, and international laws. International means including more than one nation. Officers no longer patrol on horseback.

RCMP officers only wear their red uniforms for special events.

Instead, they use cars, boats, and aircraft. They only wear their red uniforms for special events. Officers wear dark blue uniforms for everyday police work.

The RCMP preserves its past through its Musical Ride program. The Musical Ride program is a series of public riding shows set to music. Officers wear red uniforms and perform riding drills. The drills show the riding skills that early officers used each day in the territories.

Chapter 3

Mounted Officers

Officers in mounted units perform everyday police work and they work with horses. Working with horses is not always easy. Officers must stay in control of their horses on busy city streets. They must watch for possible dangers to their horses.

Officers volunteer to serve on most mounted units. Any officer with patrol experience can volunteer. But unit leaders look for officers with certain qualities.

Unit leaders prefer volunteers who have experience with horses. But experience is not necessary. Successful volunteers must care about animals. They must be patient and understanding. They must also care about people.

Volunteers must care about animals and people.

Trainees learn how to use their horses to control crowds.

Officers who join mounted units attend training courses. Some units have their own training programs. Others send officers to private training schools. Most training programs last one to two weeks. Officers also receive training on the job.

Officer Training
Officer trainees learn many skills during their training. A trainee is a person who is in training.

Some of the training occurs in classrooms. Most of the training occurs on horseback.

Trainees receive basic training first. They learn to get on and off horses. They learn how to sit on horses. Trainees also learn how to control the gait of horses. A gait is the way a horse walks or runs.

Officer trainees learn advanced riding skills after they know basic skills. They learn how to stay in saddles when horses jump or rear. Rear means to rise up on the hind legs. Trainees learn how to ride at night and on city streets.

Trainees learn how to use their horses for police work. They learn how to shoot and make arrests while on horseback. Trainees learn how to search for and rescue people. They also learn how to control crowds.

Trainees learn how to select police horses that suit them. They learn about riding equipment and how to care for their horses. They also learn how to desensitize their horses. Desensitize means to make a horse used to noises and people. Desensitizing prepares horses for the sounds and confusion of busy city streets.

Chapter 4

Police Horses

Mounted units acquire their horses in different ways. Some units use police department funds to buy horses. Other units use money given to them by people and groups. People may also give horses to the units.

Not every horse is suitable for police work. Only one out of 10 horses has the right qualities. Police horses should be within certain age, size, and weight ranges. They must be calm and obedient. Obedient means willing to follow commands.

Physical Requirements

Most mounted units prefer new horses that are three to four years old. Young horses tend to be stronger and braver than older horses. They are also easier to train. Most mounted units want

Only one out of 10 horses is right for police work.

horses that are three to nine years old. But some units accept horses that are as old as fifteen. Many units prefer horses that are brown or chestnut. Chestnut is a dark shade of brown.

Units look for horses that are at least five and one-half feet (1.65 meters) tall. People measure the height of a horse from the ground to a horse's shoulders. Units prefer horses that are nine feet (2.7 meters) or longer from nose to tail. They also prefer horses that weigh 1,100 to 1,300 pounds (495 to 585 kilograms).

These horses can support riders easily. Officers sit up higher on larger horses. This gives them a better view of their surroundings. Larger horses also give officers a powerful appearance.

Breeds

Some horse breeds are better suited for police work than others. But most mounted units cannot be too selective. They select the best breeds they can afford. They also choose the best horses from those given to them. This means most units include many breeds of horses.

Two common breeds include the American quarter horse and the saddlebred horse. Both breeds are strong horses with powerful muscles

Many mounted units prefer horses that are brown or chestnut.

and good stamina. Stamina is the energy and strength to do something for a long time. They are calm and they adapt well to most situations. Most of these horses are brown and chestnut.

Other breeds include thoroughbreds, morgans, and Tennessee walkers. Thoroughbreds are the fastest breed of horses. They pay attention to their surroundings and they learn quickly. Morgans are strong and have a great deal of stamina. Tennessee walkers have smooth, graceful gaits. Most Tenneessee walkers are brown or chestnut.

Trainers desensitize horses by waving objects in front of the horses' eyes.

Mixed-breed horses are the most common horses in police units. A mixed-breed horse is the offspring of two different breeds. Many mixed-breed horses are sturdy and dependable. They come in many colors.

Testing Period

Horses go through test periods before they become full-time police horses. The test periods last at least 30 days. Mounted units use test periods to decide whether horses can handle work on city streets.

Some test periods include off-street tests and street tests. Trainers desensitize horses during off-street tests. Officers ride horses on patrols during street tests.

Trainers desensitize horses by exposing them to the sights and sounds of cities. The trainers wave objects in front of the horses' eyes. They play recordings of gunshots, loud music, and street sounds.

Trainers do not hurt the horses. The training is necessary so the horses do not become scared on the street. Scared horses might rear, jump, or run. They could hurt themselves, their riders, and other people.

Officers select suitable horses for street tests. The officers ride the horses on street patrol for several weeks. They watch how their horses act. Only horses that are calm and obedient pass the street tests. Mounted units do not keep horses that are nervous or hard to control. They return these horses to their original owners.

Chapter 5

Service and Duties

Officers and their horses develop strong bonds. They work closely with one another. Officers and their horses become teams. Most mounted teams spend years together on street patrol.

In large departments, mounted teams work in shifts. Some teams patrol during the day. Others patrol at night. In smaller departments, mounted teams patrol only during the day. Or they may patrol only during special events.

Street Patrol

All mounted teams perform similar patrol duties. They receive orders each day to patrol certain areas. Some patrol parks. Others patrol

All mounted officers perform similar patrol duties.

Mounted officers put tickets on cars that are parked illegally.

neighborhoods. Some patrol busy downtown
streets.

Mounted teams are clearly visible. Their
presence helps prevent crime. Most days on street
patrol are routine. Routine means ordinary and
without problems. Mounted officers direct traffic.
They put tickets on cars that are parked illegally.
They spend time talking with people on
the streets.

Some days are not routine. Mounted teams may have to help break up crowds. They may have to stop fights. Mounted teams may help search for missing people. They might have to chase suspects. A suspect is a person believed to have committed a crime.

Riding Dangers

Horses need time to get used to new patrol areas. This is true even after the test period. Sights, sounds, and smells change daily in many patrol areas.

Mounted officers are patient. They let their horses experience the changing surroundings. They do not become angry if their horses are frightened. Instead, officers calm their horses with encouraging words and firm commands.

Riding in cities is dangerous for horses. They may have trouble walking on some city surfaces. Blacktop roads and cement sidewalks can be slippery. Sometimes these surfaces have holes in them. Horses can stumble if they are moving too quickly. Horses can even break their legs.

Most mounted units follow gait guidelines because of these dangers. The guidelines say that officers can only gallop or canter their horses in

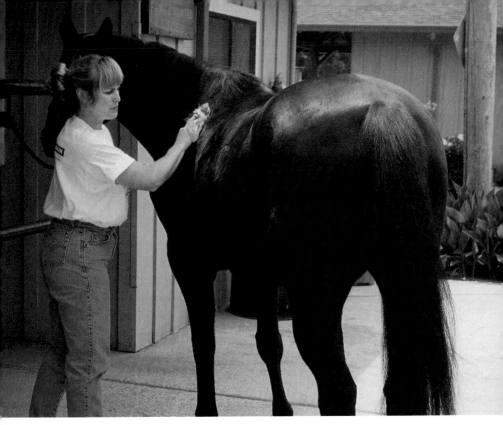

Some officers groom their own horses.

special situations. A gallop is a fast, running gait. A canter is a slower, running gait. The special situations include chasing suspects or handling emergencies.

Horse Care

Horse care is part of daily service. Mounted officers are responsible for the safety and care of their horses. The motto of all mounted units is:

The Horse Comes First. A motto is a word or saying that states what people believe.

Officers take care of their horses each day. They help feed and groom their horses. Groom means to clean and brush an animal. Officers also watch their horses for signs of sickness. They help their horses overcome fears.

Feeding and Grooming

Mounted officers in some units are responsible for feeding and grooming their horses. Hostlers help officers in other units. A hostler is a person who is trained in the care of horses.

Officers or hostlers feed horses twice a day. The horses may receive hay and oats. Or they may eat manufactured horse food. On patrol, officers make sure no one feeds their horses. But some officers give their horses snacks.

Mounted officers or hostlers groom their horses at least once each day. They use curry combs and body brushes. The combs and brushes untangle hair in the horses' coats. They remove sweat and dirt. Combing and brushing also relaxes the horses' stiff muscles.

Checking a horse's hooves is another important grooming task. Horses pick up small stones and other objects in their hooves. These objects could cause the horses to become sick. They could even cause the horses to become lame. Lame means unable to walk. Officers and hostlers remove these objects.

Health

Mounted officers must watch their horses closely for signs of sickness. It is not always obvious when horses are sick or in pain.

Veterinarians treat sick horses. A veterinarian is a doctor for animals. Veterinarians also give horses shots. The shots protect horses from some sicknesses.

Officers leave their horses in the stables on icy or very rainy days. Icy or wet streets can be difficult for horses to walk on. It is also hard for drivers to see mounted teams on very rainy days. This can increase the chances for accidents.

Officers check horses' hooves for small stones and other objects.

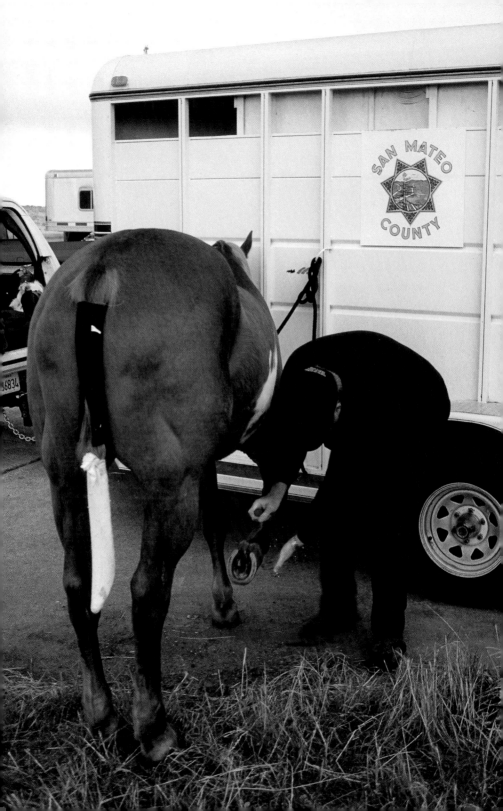

Bridle

Reins

Mounted Team

Riding Hat

Pepper Spray

Riding Pants

Saddlebag

Saddle

Stirrup

Chapter 6

Equipment

Mounted police work requires special equipment. The equipment includes all the tools and gear necessary for riding horses. It also includes tools and gear needed for police work.

Tack and Saddlebags

Tack is the most important riding equipment. Mounted officers sit on horses and control their movement with tack. Tack includes the saddle and bridle. A bridle is a system of straps. The straps fit around a horse's head and mouth. Reins are part of each bridle. Stirrups hang from each saddle. Stirrups are devices that hold a rider's feet.

Many officers use saddlebags. A saddlebag hangs across the back of a horse behind the saddle. Officers use saddlebags to hold things such as their ticket books.

Stirrups hold riders' feet.

Mounted officers' uniforms have not changed much since 1871.

Horseshoes

Horses wear horseshoes to protect their hooves from the hard ground. Horseshoes are U-shaped pieces of iron. Blacksmiths fasten them to the bottom of a horse's hooves. A blacksmith is a person skilled at making things out of iron.

Horses in mounted units receive special horseshoes. Their shoes have cleats. Cleats are small lumps of metal on the bottom of a horseshoe. Cleats give horses better footing on hard or slippery surfaces.

Uniforms

Mounted officers wear special uniforms. Most uniforms include riding pants, leather boots, spurs, and crops. The uniforms have not changed much since 1871.

Officers' riding pants and boots help make riding more comfortable. Horses often rub against objects like cars, buildings, and trees. The boots and pants protect officers' legs and feet from these objects.

Most mounted officers wear spurs on their boots. Spurs are small, metal wheels. Officers also carry crops. A crop is a small, stick-like whip. Officers use their spurs to gently nudge horses that will not move. Or they tap the horses with their crops.

Different mounted units use different-colored uniforms. Dark blue is the most common color. Some units use lighter shades of blue. Other units have brown, gray, or green uniforms.

Police Belts, Hats, and Helmets

All mounted officers wear thick, leather police belts. The belts hold officers' weapons and bullets. They also hold two-way radios, handcuffs, and pepper spray. Pepper spray causes a burning feeling in the eyes and the lungs. Pepper spray is not deadly. It allows mounted officers to control suspects without using weapons.

Officers wear hats for everyday patrol work. Some officers wear wide-brimmed cowboy hats. Some wear police caps. Others wear police hard hats.

Most officers also carry helmets on their saddles. Officers put the helmets on when they control crowds. Some helmets have clear face shields. The helmets protect officers' heads and faces.

Weapons

Sometimes mounted officers have to use weapons to protect the public, themselves, and their horses. Mounted officers carry batons and handguns. A baton is a small wooden club. Batons help officers stop suspects or control violent people.

Most mounted officers have semi-automatic handguns. Semi-automatic handguns are small but powerful guns that fire bullets quickly. Each semi-automatic handgun holds 15 to 17 bullets.

Mounted officers carry handguns and batons.

Years of Patrol

Officers and their horses often work together for many years. They work to make cities safer places to live. Most mounted teams serve together for at least 10 years. Some mounted teams have patrolled streets for as long as 18 years.

Mounted units retire horses that can no longer perform patrol work. Most mounted units have adoption programs for their retired horses. Sometimes officers adopt their own horses. Sometimes citizens adopt the horses. Some mounted units have farms. Their retired horses spend the rest of their lives on these farms.

Words to Know

baton (buh-TON)—a small wooden club

blacksmith (BLAK-smith)—a person skilled at making things out of iron

bridle (BRYE-duhl)—a system of straps that fits around a horse's head and mouth

carriage (KAIR-ij)—a small, two-wheeled car.

chestnut (CHEST-nught)—a dark shade of brown

crop (KROP)—a small, stick-like whip

deputy (DEP-yoo-tee)—a law enforcement officer who works for a sheriff

desensitize (dee-SEN-suh-tize)—to make a horse used to noises and people

gait (GATE)—the way a horse walks or runs

groom (GROOM)—to clean and brush an animal

hostler (HOST-luhr)—a person who is trained in the care of horses

international (in-tur-NASH-uh-nuhl)—including more than one nation

motto (MOT-oh)—a word or saying that states what people believe

pepper spray (PEP-ur SPRAY)—a spray that causes a burning feeling in the eyes and the lungs

province (PROV-uhnss)—a region similar to a state

rear (rihr)—to rise up on the hind legs

spurs (SPURS)—small, metal wheels worn on boots

stable (STAY-buhl)—a barn for horses

stamina (STAM-uh-nuh)—the energy and strength to do something for a long time

suspect (suh-SPEKT)—a person believed to have committed a crime

tack (TAK)—equipment used to control the movement of horses; includes the saddle and bridle

trainee (tray-NEE)—a person who is in training

transportation (transs-pur-TAY-shuhn)—all the ways of moving people and goods

veterinarian (vet-ur-uh-NER-ee-uhn)—a doctor for animals

volunteer (vol-uhn-TIHR)—to offer to do a job

To Learn More

Demuth, Jack. *City Horse*. New York: Dodd Mead, 1979.

Kallen, Stuart A. *The Police Station*. Minneapolis: Abdo and Daughters, 1997.

Winkleman, Katherine K. *Police Patrol*. New York: Walker and Company, 1996

Wirths, Claudine G. *Choosing a Career in Law Enforcement*. New York: Rosen Publishing Group, 1996.

Useful Addresses

**New York City Police Department
   Mounted Unit**
621 West 42nd Street
New York, NY 10036

Royal Canadian Mounted Police
1200 Vanier Parkway
Ottawa, ON K1A 0R2
Canada

**San Jose Police Department
   Mounted Unit**
2525 Kenoga Drive
San Jose, CA 95121

Internet Sites

International Museum of the Horse
http://www.imh.org/

New York Police Department
http://www.ci.nyc.ny.us/html/nypd/

NYPD Police Patches
http://www.vdot.net/~jvb091/policeworks/nypd/
   nypd.html

RCMP Main Page
http://www.rcmp-grc.gc.ca/html/rcmp2.htm

Mounted officers and their horses work together on
patrol for many years.

Index